I0162209

RAW EMOTIONS OF A DREAMER...

Josephine Alon

RAW EMOTIONS OF A DREAMER...

Josephine Alon

Poetry

Cover: Baruch Elron

Drawings: Ion Vincent Danu

ISBN: 978 0-359-56563-4

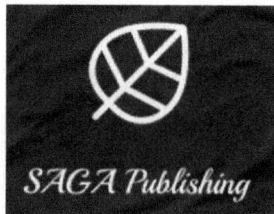

SAGA Publishing

Gentle soul of a poet…

Gentle soul of a poet
lost in time
amongst the verses
seeking sweet inspiration
for a poem.

From the realm of raw emotions
spilling out of his dreams
he creates a magic poem,
and from a myriad of thoughts
lines fly on the horizon
like a Condor on the wind.

It is the destiny of poets
to be captive of raw beauty
in a quest of endless love
for divine poetry.

(2014)

I am excited just to be...

I am excited just to be
a sweet smile on your lips
in the twilight of the end of time.

I am excited just to be
the fragrance of the flowers
enchanted by the mystery of life.

I am excited just to be
an actor on the stage of love
a fluid image dreaming next to thee.

I am excited just to be
engulfed by burning passion
when you are making love to me.

I am excited just to be
a feather in the purple winds
flying in between the fluffy clouds.

I am excited just to be
a fire fly on summer nights
blessed by the Moon and many stars.
I am excited just to be...

(2016)

The game of love...

From the balcony of life
I sighted you
amongst the millions of faces
whilst intensive fire
scorched my soul.

I knew,
you were the only one for me,
a troubadour
from many dreams of wonder
lured by the Cupid
of the winds.

Drenched by light of a rising sun
and in a rupture of emotions,
both our souls intertwined to play
the game of love...

(2016)

I cherish life...

I cherish life
with all of its shifting colours
and the gentle turning of its seasons.

I cherish life
with early mornings
covered by silver drops of dew.

I cherish life
when nights inspire
sinful love and pleasurable pursuits.

I cherish life
when spring arrives
melting the ice from frozen hearts.

I cherish life
when you are smiling,
telling me I am the only one!

I cherish life...

(2017)

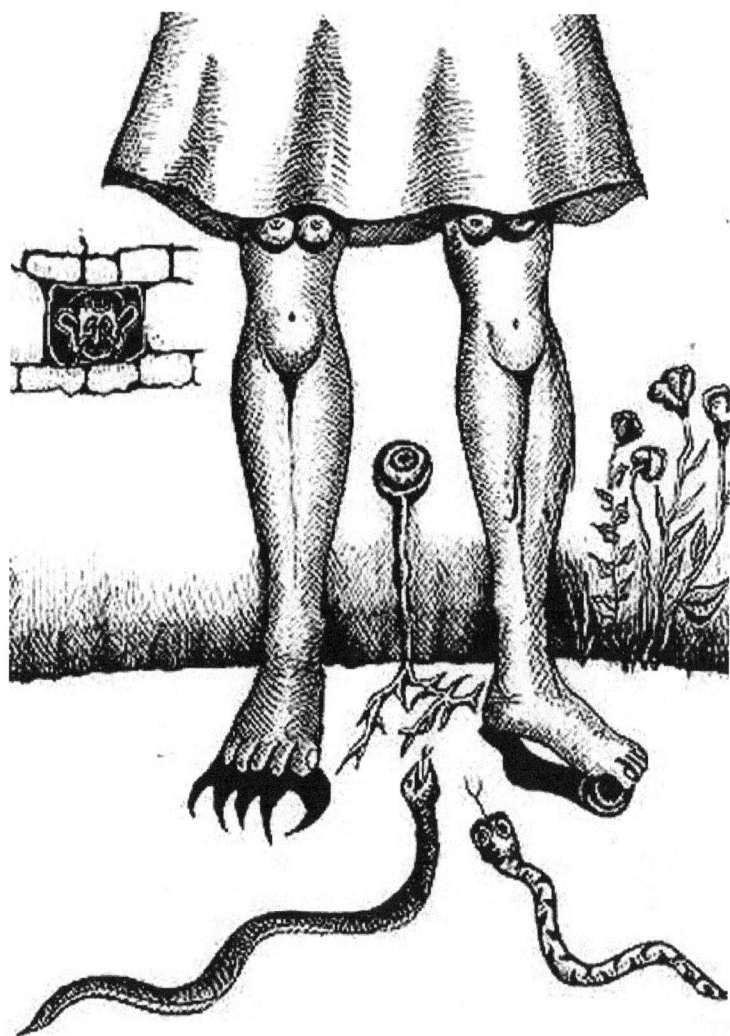

The resolve of youth...

I am at the cross roads of my life,
a defining moment of confusion
not knowing what to do.

My vibrant past it holds me back
and a heavy fog embraces my future
jolting my being.

And yet I still pursue my dreams
and if I get lost at times
yes, I will try again.

There are many bridges to be crossed.
I am on a journey with detours
with the resolve of youth.

(2014)

Dreaming Away

Swamped by distant memories
and overwhelming thoughts
I ask myself if I could save
my love for you.

Through pores exuding sadness
and shattered pale illusions,
I struggled with despair
to reach you.

Kept prisoner by distant sensibility
I pensively sit on life's veranda
with a steaming cup of coffee
dreaming away.

(2018)

Love is my wine...

Fragile leaves have fallen yet
in a dance of autumn passion
scattering in the winds.

A rusty shade of a changing season
inspires all my senses
and I breathe just love.

Touched by the ecstasy of Bacchus
patchy memories are hazy
love, it is my wine.

Drunk from the cup of love
lost, I feel a torrid passion,
a blessing from above.

Hanging from the cords of heaven
serenaded by the stars
I succumb to you.

(2014)

Thoughts of Love...

Love is like a Fata Morgana,
a mirage
amongst the moving sands
where senses
are hopelessly seduced
sending the heart aflutter
then disappearing
over the vast horizon
in a purple blazing glory.

And if a few droplets of rain
fall upon the imaginary dunes,
the rainbow illuminates the sky
with sparkles of a hope
which gives one courage
to love again!

(2013)

Spring

The symphony of white and green,
the fragile snow drop petals
allow their crown to be seen
as spring gently settles.

Translucent little stars of ice
of intricate and fine lace
are melting on the window glass
as winter leaves with grace.

The sweet fragrance of spring
makes me feel young once again

I wish to dream, to laugh, to sing
forgetting winter's pain.

My nostrils breathe in new sensations
the atmosphere is full of joy.
Around me are sweet temptations
that are exciting to enjoy.

Euphoric songs and blinding sun
returning birds of luscious colours
new hopes, and lots of fun
and fields covered by many flowers.

Twittering birds on blossomed trees
spreading the joy of loving
beautiful butterflies, restless bees,
with happiness are buzzing.

The spell of spring, it makes me giddy
I want to be in love again
my frozen heart is very needy
I wish to dream and be insane.

(2012)

Good morning life...

I hesitate to leave the night behind
when dreams are swinging
from the fragile strings
of darkness...

I linger in a fluid film of scattered thoughts
I ponder if I shouldn't let them go
to fade into the rising sun.

Your foggy image from the dream of dreams
it slowly drifts into the morning light
and you are gone.

Good morning life...

(2018)

Purple fantasies and dreams...

Purple fantasies and dreams
have vanished into memory
enveloped by the fumes
from old flames
of now gone
out.

Remains of the black debris
are settling upon the hopes,
and empty dreams
are fading into
the heavy
fog.

Most fantasies and dreams
are dancing all around
a much deeper truth,
becoming flitting
shadow of
nefarious
pursuits.

(2017)

Sweet Mermaid...

Sweet mermaid from the
ocean
lose yourself in my embrace
with the deepest of emotions
melting into each other's grace.

Choreographing magic love
in a dance of full seduction

and with only the sky
above
sinking in each other's
passion.

Lost in the fire of the
moment
and engulfed with no
appeal
in surroundings, totally
absent
only love is what I
feel.

Shiny stars appear in the
sky
diamonds with angel
faces,
happy in love, wishing to
cry
lose my dear in my
embraces.

(2013)

Searching for you...

Blinded by fragmented hopes
I searched for you
my soul mate.

I've chased you through
so many hazy dreams
where love
is paving old forgotten
alleys.

This was the place
I wished to reignite the spark of love
and light the fire in your soul
but I was wrong.
No sign of you,
elusive soul mate…

(2013)

Morning dew...

A gust of winds is sweeping
beneath the door of my imagination
distorting my perceptions.

Scattered emotions of love and hate
colour my restless dreams
which seem so real.

Through heavy, misty fog
I see your superfluous image,
a passing illusion that haunts me.

I know it is a nightmare
and strongly I protest with shrills
that pierce the silence of the night.

"Be gone" I say to the nightmares,
"I seek morning's dew".

(2014)

I am seduced...

I am seduced
by the sweet whisper
of the wind in my ears
a melody of hope
and only me
to listen
under the restless clouds
of my life.

Whilst captured
by the gentle tune,
I softly hum the song
inspired by the love
for life and you.

(2016)

My soul mate...

Rambling winds of loneliness
are sneaking by the window
of my destiny.

Beguiled into some elusive hopes,
relentlessly I look for you,
my soul mate.

I am chasing dreams by the river's bank
where willow trees are chanting
and the sun cuddles alleys.

Here is the place I like to find you
within the momentary sparks
and the fortitude of love.

(2016)

Love in spring

Restrained emotions yearn to fly,
arousing so many senses,
the thrill of love reaches the sky
on wings of purple verses.

Unruly thoughts bound together
like a bouquet of flowers
ornate my soul, lace of light
a rainbow of amazing colours.

Excited by spring's attraction
and all the hugs from rays of sun,
consumed I am by sweet passion,
ruptured emotions, lots of fun.

Entangled in lost dreams of love,
gently I spread my fragile wings
and pray from my heart, to the sky above
for sweet hopes the future brings.

(2018)

I love this dream...

The man I wish for is only in my dreams.
He is a fluid image, an elusive phantom,
somebody I could love.

A deceptive dream like all others
the image is a fantasy of youth
with vivid colours
laced by a divine tune which slowly
fades away at morning light.

My heart pulsates again with passion
then I am swept away by floods
of wild desire.

The flames inside my soul glow,
glimmering like plumes of birds
of paradise that flutter their sensuous
salacious love...

I love this dream...

(2016)

I am a complex Algorithm...

I am a complex algorithm
from far away star dust
finely tuned by evolution
but stifled by the rules of life
and by the many questions
I do have.

My mind travels
between the constellations
with the speed of light,
and with my dreams
I wander the universe
avoiding life's meteorites.

I can't avoid them all
and some will crush my soul
yet I remain a complex algorithm
from far away star dust...

(2017)

Ocean in love...

Driven by the joy of the living
and the rumbling of the ocean
I am wondering
what its waves will bring
from beyond the shores.

Maybe an old bottle
with a faded yellow note
or some opalescent shells,
offerings from Mother Nature
laid with love on golden sands.

On a cruise of fantasy
mesmerised I watch the ocean
that embraces the sandy shores
with perpetual devotion.

(2013)

The Spring in my soul...

A mosaic of emotions
with its many shades of love
is pouring from my soul.

Perhaps it is the season
that gives me all the reason
to fall in love again.

The trees are in full blossom
amazing beams of colour
a fantasy of spring.

The sunny rays are dazzling
I reach for their warm blessing
and I am happy.

(2018)

My inner child...

My sweet angel, my inner child,
with curls in the winds of time
innocent eyes that sparkle
in the darkness of the night
with tears of sorrow.

My sweet angel, my inner child
never too late to wipe away
your tears and images
engraved in the memory
of a bitter childhood.

My sweet angel, my inner child
I wish to heal your crying soul
to take your suffering away
embracing you
with endless
love.

My sweet angel, my inner child
do spread your agile wings
and fly to promising horizons
a blessed haven
full of hope.

(2016)

Imagination...

My rich imagination
hangs from the fluffy clouds
at times, it rides on puffy dreams.

It flirts with inspiration
gliding in - between the stars
in total abandon, so light, ebullient.

A real rupture of the senses
it feels surreal, it is like heaven
It captures raw and wild emotions.

It listens to the winds,
and with love it hugs the rainbow
then spreads its wings and soars...

(2016)

The whisper of the winds...

I listen to the whisper of the winds.
It is a song of hope and love
under the restless clouds.

I am seduced by its magical sound
and I am hum it softly
just for myself.

I drift away to the land of fantasy
feeling the rupture of all senses.
I am in heaven.

Please come with me my only love
lets dream again whilst listening
to the whisper of the winds.

(2016)

Sure, I will try again...

I am at the cross-roads of my life
I feel confused not knowing
which way to go.

It feels like the past is holding back
and heavy fog embraces the future
when I am on my way.

Great distances, long bridges
are difficult to cross now
I stumble on each stone.

And yet I still pursue my dreams
and if I am getting lost at times,
sure I will try again.

(2017)

The Nightingale...

You were an intruder in my life - a nightingale,
celestial creation
with the voice of an angel.

Through a screen of heavy fog
I see you now with broken wings,
defeated by emotions.

You ceased to sing
the song I loved,
that fame long gone
forgotten in a dream,
late game in an alley paved with sorrow.

(2013)

Le fusain
crayon —
excellent
pour des
croquis rapides,
tout tremble
pour les portraits
l'ommage qu'il soit...

Léa
"clown"

Memories

Phantoms of the past are hanging
heavy from the corners of my mind,
and in the shadows of the night,
I feel engulfed
by fumes of sadness.

From the foliage of time,
I fail to recall
sweet images of forgotten kisses,
crazy memories from youth
that are leaving for their orbits.

You appear in vivid dreams
an eerie phantom in the mist
touching my face, as gentle breeze
to my memories I surrender.

(2016)

Shameful game...

I do not wish to play your petty games
where you are lying and I guess
whether it is true or not.

Entwined with human frailty my gentle spirit
is engulfed by waves of sadness
and a tsunami of emotions.

Crushed and distressed my soul crumbles;
tears are hanging from my lashes
I am overwhelmed by grief.

So many shadows are now in between us
pale face of your indiscretions
which bruise my soul.

You shattered all my dreams and hopes
leaving behind only shredded feelings
laced with the frills of sadness.

I wish now to move on with my life
and shine in the glint of the sun
embracing rays of hope.

(2018)

Prospect for the future...

Lost, I am wandering through the web of many links
and algorithms, and between maths equations
which rule the Cyber.

It feels so lonely, only me and my computer
the solitude hovering above my shoulders,
and there is no smell of fresh cut grass
or summer breeze that sways branches on the trees.

Virtual flowers are growing on the screen
but I cannot feel their sweet perfume
or touch their velvet petals.

And you my love, a cold and elusive image,
devoid of deep feelings is floating
aimlessly on the web.

Cyber technology is claiming all my senses.
It rips them from our souls
deleting or archiving them
somewhere
in the Clouds.

Riding on the crest of time
"viruses" are celebrating
erasing all my files.

Ooops...

Reflections on my life...

When the final act is almost finished
and heavy velvet curtains fall,
I ask myself what I've accomplished
in Josephina's role.

A complex role with lengthy bridges,
that many times I had to cross,
climbing on top of mountain ridges
trying to be my own boss.

I grabbed at life with both my hands
and I refused to leave on cue
enjoyed the world of many lands,
I lived my life the best I knew.

I loved, I cried, I felt betrayed
but no regrets, I lived in full
I chose my way and never strayed
abiding by my own rules.

As the final act is almost finished
and velvet curtains slowly fall,
I feel my life is well accomplished
in Josephina's role.

(2013)

Unsettled souls...

There are unsettled souls who believe
we live forever
some dreams come alive
some never
illusions followed by so many fears
washed down
by time and by salty tears.

There are unsettled souls who
believe
that everything in life is nothing
and love
is tumbles into insignificance
being painted
in the colour of the brass
only to become
a sad and a confusing farce.

There are unsettled souls who
believe
that fantasies and dreams are real,
and still,
their views are written into
the sand
with rules they would not ever
bend.

There are unsettled souls...

(2018)

I am flirting...

I am flirting with nostalgic thoughts
faded in the recesses of my mind.
Perhaps I miss the years of youth
gone like the snow in spring, or maybe
I am missing lost dreams
covered with heavy dust.

Nostalgic, I embrace the years bygone
that once seduced my needy soul
a wondering traveller along
the rocky roads.

I don't regret the past
and with serenity
I hug new rays of hope
which flicker
through the cracks
of gloomy moments.

I'm flirting with nostalgic thoughts...

(2016)

Elusive Love...

I walked against the winds of time,
which pinched my bony cheeks
and made me cry.

I felt like Don Quixote of La Mancha
fighting life's windmills
of an elusive love.

I clung from futile rays of hope,
consumed by a corrosive love
and crouching in the corner.

There are insane deluded follies
thinly veiled by youth's dreams
and the fantasies of omnipotence.

And through the window of the past,
still up against some raw emotions,
I wonder if you ever loved me...

(2016)

Free Fall...

I walk like in a dream
with my injured soul stranded
at the junction of my life
where ways are paved
with casualties
of love
and
hate.

I try to navigate through life.
It makes me ill to see
there are no ways for me
to heal, and I don't know
if to go or stay,

whether to cry
or
pray.

Feelings of dread over take my being
when a dark shadow
covers my once blue sky
and I plummet like a stone
in an emotional free fall,
free fall, free fall,
free
fall.

(2014)

I let my past go...

I let my past go!
Forgotten is the old road,
but not the burning passion
I have for life.

I am desensitised
from surrogate emotions,
or any old blinkers
I used to wear during
my fragile youth.

With care
I stroll through memories,
forever mystified
by life's enigmatic skills
to perform illusions.

Hence, I let the past go,
to dissipate
beyond
the vast horizon.

(2019)

Complexity of love...

The weeds of sadness
grow roots within my lonely soul,
so very deep into my broken heart.

I try to flip fortune in my favour,
brave like the powerful Samson
before Delilah cut his hair.

But I am not like Samson
or devious as beautiful Delilah.
I am just a woman touched by love.

Often I hang from the hazy clouds
lost like a deer in the wilderness,
wondering what to do next.

Dreams that I have had are gone.
Just misty shadows are left for me.
The sparkle of the past has vanished.

The rusty shackles of my gentle soul
I should've dropped them long ago
and moved on with my life.

Now, slowly, I am sobering
I know life's road is full of potholes,
but I am ready for the challenge.

(2015)

Autumn

I slowly walk down on my street
crushing the leaves under my feet,
it's Autumn.

The trees are naked, a little shy,
the birds just left, adieu, goodbye
it's Autumn.

Light fog covers the trees,
embracing all my memories,
it's Autumn.

Please sweet memories don't go,
that's all I have and I know so,
It's Autumn.

It's cold and windy, and starts to rain
I chase for love, I chase in vain,
it's Autumn.

You promise to come back in spring.
I try to laugh; I try to sing,
although it's Autumn.

Until next spring I walk the street,
crushing the leaves under my feet,
it's still just Autumn.

(2016)

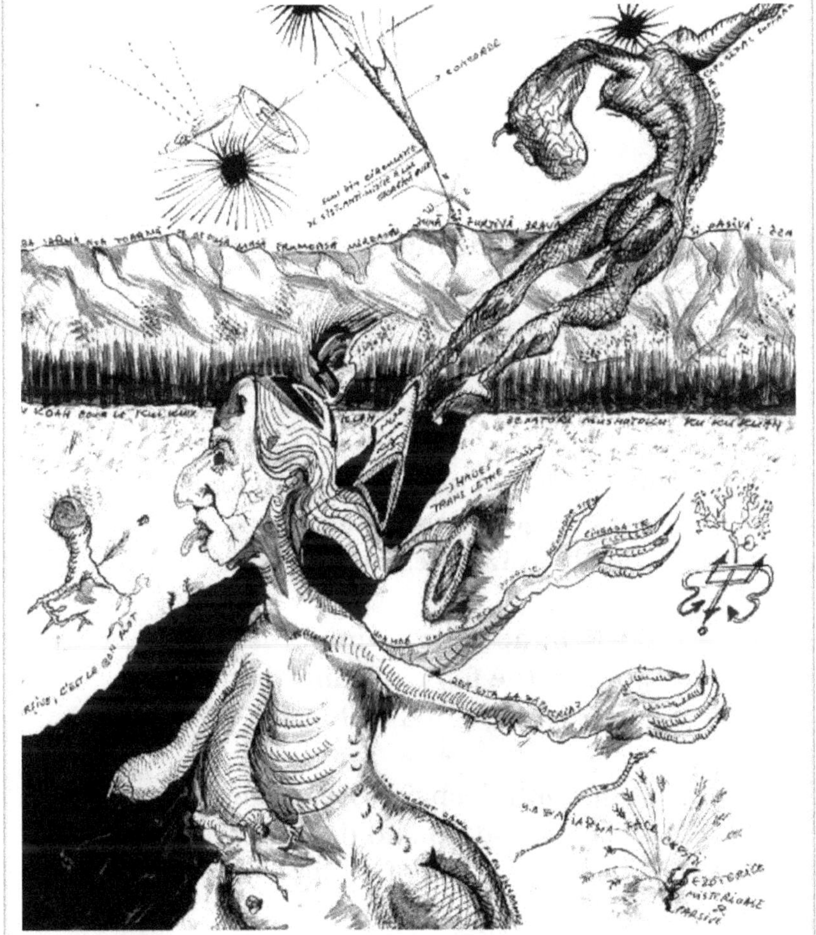
HADES
TRANS LETHE

Options...

Grafted dreams in our makeup,
enduring feelings delicately woven
into templates made of concrete.

From a myriad of tempting options
you eagerly may pitch upon,
flexible branches in the wind.

Yet, when the wrong winnow is used
wrapped in the fog that ruins dreams,
the future could be bleak...

But don't despair, love again.
Move on, stand up and do not break
as life is full of options

(2016)

A fantasy of seasons ...

A leaf fell from autumnal tree, settling on the shoulder of the lonely old man, seated on a bench in the park.

Startled, the old man gently took the dry leaf in the hollow of his palms and in wonder he watched it crumble and disappeared between his trembling fingers. Then, with sadness, he peered, shilly-shally, through the slightly opened window of his patchy memories, flush flooding his frail existence.

Griped by fragrant feelings, deeply engraved in his soul and mind, he stood up from the bench, watched in disbelief at the remains of the lifeless leaf upon the damp and cold earth where an elusive image appeared and then vanished.

"It was HER," the old man muttered softly to himself.
She was the love of his life, the only one. Yet, he never told her.
Though the idealized vision wasn't there anymore he tried to grab at it, to no avail...

"Do not leave me again, my love! Please do not," he begged...

On a wave of hazy memories, the old man slowly bent from his aching waist and picked up the few pieces of the remaining rusty leaf. With much care, he put them into the pocket of his thick woollen coat.

Fine drops of rain started to fall mingling with the salty tears escaping the old man's eyes and rolling down his face, beaten by the cruel winds of time. As if in a trance, with shuffling steps, he continued his journey through the dense fog of life...

"Wait my love, please don't go" she begged him in a muted wail.

"Remember? Do you remember the rich emerald shades of the horizon at the beginnings of spring or the promises of all-consuming love, the first stolen kiss, the first embrace and the rapid pounding of our hearts? Or maybe you remember the hot summer nights cooled by the gentle breeze and the both of us, embraced in total abandon under the fragrant Linden trees. You may remember the cold, blistering winter that we hardly felt, as the flames from our burning love kept us warm.
Do you remember, she insisted with desperation? Do you?"

But the old man was painfully oblivious to her lamentations.

"Adieu my love, adieu, she said with deep sorrow."

A sudden gust of wind blew away more rusty leaves from the autumnal tree covering the damp cold earth.

Undisturbed by the unfolding drama around him, a baby squirrel was munching on a fallen acorn.

A city, a park, a bench and two parallel worlds destined to meet again...

(2014)

Dedication

I dedicate this book in memory of my parents, Sara and Rubin.
A special dedication to a great friend of mine Hermina.

Acknowledgements

I would like to thank Adrian Grauenfels, Dana Alon and Jonty Borenstein. There would have been no book without them. Many thanks also to Sue Genziuk, Ben Borenstein and Henri Alon, my husband, for their great support.

INDEX

Gentle soul of a poet... 3

I am excited just to be... 5

The game of love 7

I cherish life... 8

The resolve of youth...11

Dreaming Away 12

Love is my wine... 14

Thoughts of Love... 15

Spring..16

Good morning life... 18

Purple fantasies and dreams....................................19

Sweet Mermaid... 20

Searching for you... 22

Morning dew... 23

I am seduced...24

My soul mate...25

Love in spring 26

I love this dream...27

I am a complex Algorithm..29

Ocean in love... 30

The Spring in my soul... 31

My inner child...32

Imagination..34

The whisper of the winds... 35

Sure, I will try again... 36

The Nightingale... 38

Memories 40

Shameful game... 41

Prospect for the future.......................................43

Reflections on my life... 46

Unsettled souls...48

I am flirting... 50

Elusive Love... 52

Free Fall... 53

I let my past go... 55

Complexity of love..57

Autumn...59

Options... 62

A fantasy of seasons 63

Josephina Alon lives with her husband, children and grandchildren in Melbourne, Australia.

Her first collection of poetry was published as a book in 2013. Her talent is remarkable, oozing from a unique inspiration. She manages to express her love for life and strong sentiments regarding romance, melancholy, nostalgia and serenity through complex and expressive writings.

Sue Genziuk

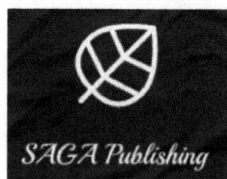
SAGA Publishing

www.ingramcontent.com/pod-product-compliance
Lightning Source LLC
Chambersburg PA
CBHW060146050426

42448CB00010B/2318